Unheard Voices - A

GW00500452

contents

Unheard Voices - *An Anthology*

Foreword

When we were appointed as Co-Writers in Residence for Clackmannanshire we were given the exciting opportunity of helping to foster creative writing in Scotland's smallest county.

In March 2007 we held our first workshop at Alloa Library and we really had no idea how many writers, if any, might turn up. Two years down the line and after scores of one-to-one meetings and dozens of creative events and practical workshops, we can confidently say that creative writing is now well and truly established in the Wee County.

The publication of 'Unheard Voices' is proof positive of the wealth of local talent which exists and we are proud of the small part we have played in its development.

We would like to make a special mention to Kathleen O'Neill and Ron Carthy at Clackmannanshire Council for their support and encouragement, to John Blake and all the library staff for their unstinting help, and to Gill Campbell and Gillian McNeish for the typesetting and proofreading. Without them, none of this would have been possible.

Most of all, thank you to all the local writers who have been involved, a selection of whose work we celebrate within these pages.

Stuart Hepburn, Tom Murray
Co-Writers in Residence
December 2008

Authors' biographies

Dave Bisio
Dave Bisio doesn't really exist. He's only part of human fertile imagination. What he appears to create is only done to confuse alien life forms.

Julie Rose Clark
Previous winner of a poetry prize in Huddersfield Literature Festival in 2008. The author has had several of her poems published and self-published a volume of poetry in 2002 entitled ' I Like You Like I Love'.

Ian Ellis
When I heard a poet recite the words 'a rat dragged its slimy belly over the waste ground' I woke up to poetry.

Tricia Golledge
Tricia Golledge 39, former international jet-setting diplomat, customer services' operative; and now wife, mother, sometime doctors' receptionist and a writer!

Paul Green
My name is Paul Green, and from the first time a pencil made sense to me I've been writing short stories.

Jim Kean
Originally from Lanarkshire, Jim has lived in the Hillfoots for over 20 years and took up writing as a hobby in 2007 following a winter break in the sun.

Rosa Macpherson
Rosa Idziak Macpherson was born and raised in Alloa. Recipient of an SAC Writers Bursary her work has appeared in numerous anthologies and broadcast on radio.

James Watters McKean
James Watters McKean lives in Sauchie. He was educated at Lornshill Academy, despite which, he graduated in English and is currently reading for a Masters in English Literature.

Mike Mitchell
Writing poetry and short stories since the mid-seventies; published in several Scottish literary magazines and Poetry Scotland (#47). Cerebral rather than Nature.

Jo Ross
Joanne Ross was first published in 2000, in Cutting Teeth Glasgow and went on to have several short plays produced at the Traverse Theatre, Edinburgh.

Leela Sanchdev
Leela Sanchdev, born in Kampala, lives in Alloa and calls Scotland home. She taught History and Modern Studies at a local Comprehensive.

Jane M Spence
With fond memories of my playmates male and female living in the brick building in Erskine Street in the 1920's. All have gone but myself.

Stefano Turato
Stefano Turato is an architect who lives in Alloa with his wife Caroline and two children, Chiara and Luca. He is currently writing a novel.

The Last House
by Gavin Broom

Mr Wolfe's letter arrived on time at five past eight in the morning, just after the news had finished on the radio. As usual, the clatter of the letterbox sent the dog pounding to the door in excitement and the cat scampering up the stairs in fright. As usual, I finished off my toast and orange juice before collecting the brown envelope, now speckled with dog saliva, from the hall. As usual, I assigned the correspondence straight to the bin.

There was no need to open it. I already knew its contents. It would be the same as it had been everyday for the last two months.

With this chore complete, I could get on with the next stage of my routine; Sudoku. By eight thirty, all three puzzles -- including a Super Killer -- were complete and the paper joined the unopened mail in the bin.

Then it started, just as it always did. Drills, hammers, heavy machinery; if it could make a noise, it was next door and being used to great effect. It had been like this for a fortnight, since Mr and Mrs Hayes sold up and moved on. My life of routine continued, as by eight forty five, I closed the front door behind me and began my journey to the hospital.

It was a Wednesday, so I took a break and met Mrs Sevenoaks early that afternoon. On Wednesdays, pensioners get 10% off at B&Q, and while Mrs Sevenoaks and I have never bought anything there, it's good to go for a nosey. I like to stroll round the garden centre and smell the wonderful cacophony of scents from the blooms. It reminds me of my younger, fitter days. Mrs Sevenoaks stays inside and looks at the power, because she's scared of wasps.

"Did you get your letter from Mr Wolfe today, Isobel?" she asked, later on at the cafe.

I pursed my lips and murmured as I spread some more clotted cream on my scone.

"It went straight in the bin," I explained sourly. "I don't know when that man's going to get the hint."

Mrs Sevenoaks nodded and shook her head at the same time. "I don't know, Isobel. My Charlie says he'll never give up. It's a battle of wills now, apparently."

Sometimes, Mrs Sevenoaks can forget her surroundings and she took such a greedy bite from her scone that I had to turn away and pretend to watch the goings-on out on the street. When I looked back, she had a seed from her raspberry jam lodged in her whiskers.

"It's easy for your Charlie to say that," I said. "He's long moved out now. He's got his own life, his own children. He has a future."

Mrs Sevenoaks looked appalled. "I'm sure he didn't mean anything by it, Isobel. You know my Charlie thinks the world of you." As an afterthought, she added, "And your Matthew."

"Yes, well …" I said, folding my arms tight against me.

The cafe was full with pensioners like Mrs Sevenoaks and I, most of whom I'd already said hello to in B&Q. They all had their own troubles, I'm sure. I didn't for one minute think that I was unique. The difference was, they hadn't lost their smiles. They talked of bingo games and bus trips. They regaled each other with well worn and embellished anecdotes. They kept their secrets buried. Me? Well, for me it was written all over my face. Even Mrs Sevenoaks looked unusually content, so it wasn't a shock when she made her announcement a few minutes later.

"I've decided to sell out, Isobel," she explained. "I'm accepting Mr Wolfe's offer."

I nodded. It had been a matter of time. Despite this, I had never felt so alone as I did in that cafe.

"I'd better be going now, Mrs Sevenoaks," I said, surprised that my voice hadn't lost its strength. "Visiting hours will be starting soon."

It was approaching teatime when I arrived home and Matthew's dog was asleep on the couch, in the same position he'd been in when I'd left that morning. He opened one eye to look at me and wagged his tail half-heartedly. Like us all, he wasn't getting any younger. God alone knew what that cat got up to during the day.

I put food in both bowls while I waited for the kettle to boil. It had been a tough day up at the hospital. Things had been said that couldn't be taken back and I desperately needed a cup of tea to calm my nerves.

Charlie Sevenoaks had been right. I wasn't stupid. I could complete three Sudoku in under half an hour, after all, including a Super Killer. Mr Wolfe was never going to give up. He was younger than me, he was wealthier than me and he was more evil than me. I could keep fighting it so long as I had an ally but now I was on my own, my resolve had been destroyed and the battle had been lost.

I took my time over my tea and when I was finished, I made my way up the stairs and stood at the closed door. There was a sticker on it which read, "This Room Belongs To Matthew Stone". The blue ink was fading, but I could still make it out. I opened the door and looked back in time. Fifteen years. It had remained this way while my Matthew lay up in his little room; my brave Sleeping Beauty.

"It's time now, Matty," I said aloud, despite the fact that I'd already explained all of this at the hospital. Somehow, it seemed more personal in his room. "It's time."

Downstairs, the cat came thundering through the catflap and meowed loudly, unimpressed with my choice for her dinner. I closed the door and walked back downstairs for another cup of tea.

The next day, when Mr Wolfe's letter arrived, I opened it.

A Shadow
by Ian Ellis

Eyes do not meet in dreams
In death's dream kingdom.
In this place we walk and avoid
Hoping that no one will look.
Still I yearn, but always avoid
Hoping someone will notice.
I must be in death's twilight
Where the only hope is emptiness.
Is it like this, in death's other kingdom?
Where dream's realm is all.
I was walking for a purpose
But I missed myself.
Between the idea and the act,
Between the reality and the consequence.
Between the idea and the fact,
Like a shadow, lies fear.
I walk around
Entirely alone now
And the truth is
I turned myself away.

Mither O' Twa Boys
by Kerry Butler

Whit 're yous daein?
Whit's happenin' here?
See a' this mess. See yous. See here.
Ah've no got time tae rin abuit
an' clean up a' this burach. Ah've no.

Ah watch yous rinnin,
Ah watch yous lauch
you turn an' smile with they spairklin een.
Yous brek ma hert. Yous dae, ye ken.
Ah cannae believe it, ah'm an' auld mither hen.

Leave they cupboards.
Shut that fridge door.
Stoap squashin' they tamataes oan the kitchen flair.
Whit next? Aw naw, no' again.
Can ye no' just leave them well alain?

Pit the pens up high
sae the wee man'll no get them.
Aw naw. Twae late. Get the wipes.
God help him.

Sleepy time nou.
Lay doun yer heids.
Gang aff tae sleep...stoap messin abuit.

Whit stories wull ye hae, whit sangs nou?
Yin, twa, three or forty bloody two.

At last yous settle.
The tiredness taks ower.
The breathin' slows an' yer day is o'er.
Whit's left o' mine has just begun,
But ma wines got warm an' there's nae films oan.

Fa' asleep on the sofa.
Wake up a' crabbit.
Richt...aff tae bed 'cos ye feel a' wabbit.
Nae sex again,
cos ye juist cannae manage.
Yer knackered. Yer din.
Serves ye richt fur haein' bairns when yer forty!

Whit did ye dae afore they boys?
Whit wis life like....a waste o' yer time?
Ye did loads o' naethin',
but ye thocht ye were busy.
Ye ken a' abuit it nou 'cos yer life's a richt stooshy.

Whit wald ye change
Naethin at a'.
But this heid oan a young body,
nou... that wald be braw.

The Bag
by Jo Ross

You can tell a lot about people by what they wear. The wealthy make more noise as they pass, their haughty shoes, clip clopping on the pavement. The less well off you hardly hear. Their clothes rustle by, as they walk quietly, less confident in their rubber soles. And then there's the likes of me seldom seen or heard.

But take that girl, sitting there like a princess, misplaced, in the middle of a busy pedestrian precinct. People make a lot of fuss around her, in her warm red leather gloves and her cosy fur-lined leather jacket. You can be sure she didn't sleep with a golf club last night.

The Princess is new to my patch. Check how neatly her silky hair is pulled back into a ponytail, the quaint fringe tucked under that shiny black hair band, the dainty wisps of hair flying in the wind. Passers-by, scurrying avoid me, avert their eyes towards her.

All morning, I've stood selling my paper but no one shows much interest. It could be her clothes, the stylish elephant grey slacks or the flawless complexion that's catching all the attention. But if you look closer, although this one is tanned, gleaming white teeth, perfect features, you'll spot a darkness lurking behind those eyes. The Princess is centred on the black cast-iron bench. Two colour co-ordinated telephone booths frame her back, as if designed for her. She looks as if she's sat in the middle of a carefully constructed painting.

Standing in his bustling precinct is the loneliest place. A knot tightens in the pit of my stomach as I watch young couples arm in arm, new mothers and fathers rushing, along with buggies and toddlers tugging in tow. Bigger, even happier families fly by. I smile at them all, offering a copy of my paper but they're taking no notice. I use my best Vendor's voice, still nothing, except the shrill seagulls in the sky squealing and squawking with disappointment and despair. Even the Princess ignores me.

Where did I go wrong? I remember better days. Suddenly, the clinking and clunking of cups and saucers, from the nearby café gives me a jolt. The invigorating smell of fresh coffee and newly baked bread fills my nostrils. Racing children pitter, patter in chase. The crowds are talking, some shouting I catch snippets.

"How're you?"

"No bad, yersel?"

Alas but not to me.

The Princess has a large leather carpetbag, the size of small suitcase. It matches her jacket. She also has a plastic M & S carrier bag. I hanker to go over and rest by her side but a niggling deep inside stops me. I don't know why or what but there is something contaminating that picture. The Princess sits upon her throne but that pretty face has a haunted look. She puts down her carpetbag and without removing her gloves extracts a little orange bottle and a sandwich from the M & S. The Princess bites delicately. I taste every delicious mouthful. She rests the sandwich on her knee, unscrews the bottle-top and drains the orange in one swig. Replacing the bottle top, she gathers up the rest of the sandwich and stuffs it back in the bag.

I catch her catching me staring.

"Big Issue."

The Princess nods and I watch her carefully pull up her carpetbag in one hand and rise to her feet. She drops the M & S bag, carelessly, in the street as she comes towards me.

"How much?"

"£1.50."

Her eyes are penetrating.

"Guess you don't take Switch?"

I shake my head. The Princess balances the carpetbag on one arm, freeing her other hand to open it. She's unhinging the clip. I hunt for a clue as she rakes through the well of the carpetbag. There's a hairbrush, a telephone, a pile of letters, pens, a notebook, a fold-up umbrella. She's rummaging, digging deep when I see it; a large bloodstained kitchen knife, it's unmistakable; I smell the wet blood, before she has time to pull out her purse. As she grabs the purse she covers the knife with a scarf. The purse is the size of a small clutch bag. Shaking, she opens the wrong end and displays an array of cards.

"Hang on. £1.50, you say?"

I nod. She's unzipping the front of the purse, exposing a double pouch containing a treasure trove of coins. The gloved finger pokes and prods and fishes out a two-pound coin.

"There."

My numb leathery hands struggle to find fifty pence.

"Keep the change."

"Thank you. Have a nice day."

She looks right through me, drops the purse in the bag and snaps it shut. I hear the swishing and sweeping of the road sweeper as he comes towards me with his brush and trolley. I shout at her back.

"By the way. It's an offence to carry a knife."

Without turning, she clip clops off at a high speed, in the shoes I once wore.

Interim
by Mike Mitchell

You could dance
at the end of my bed,
I could watch your hips
h y p n o t i s e,
your breasts bamboozle.

Later we could eat strawberries,
drink chilled wine from crystal
glasses that sing with light,
or, perhaps, talk
about different dances,
other places, the way sunlight
changes the colour
of the wine, your hair, my mood.

We could sit cross-legged
on voluptuous cushions,
taste chocolate on each others' mouths.
And later, perhaps...
you could dance.

HBF
by DRG

Holding your hand as we walk on the beach
the sea flows through my conscious dream
your eyes fill my heart with great power and love
your soul and mine float in the clouds above

where I can hear you for all that I see
you pledged your love only to me
my heart races when I hear your beautiful name
my life changes never to be the same

from birth your life is already entwined in mine
in life our hearts beat at the same time
your words and your soft caress mean all to me
the day you were born you set my soul free

I Used To Be You
by Jim Kean

It was his first day on the road, and his first working day for two years. Despite the miserable weather his mood was good, not even dampened by his windscreen wipers emitting that awful rubbing sound as they battled to keep the windscreen clear. The first call came through on the radio for one of the new estates that had sprung up around the county, some of them not on the maps yet, but he knew where this one was. It didn't seem that long since he had put an off-plan deposit down on the biggest house. Different world to the hovel he now called home.

He drew up outside a 4-bed detached with integral garage and brick fascia and immaculate lawn and flower bed and white framed windows with chintzy blinds. The couple came out quickly, both mid thirties, he looking distinctly uncomfortable in formal dinner suit and she being careful not to soil her new blue silk dress. They barely gave him a glance as the young executive barked out the name of the hotel. All the way there the dutiful wife received her briefing on who to talk to, who was on their way out, what to say to whom, and who she had to impress; oh, and how much she could drink. They got out and the passenger's smile was painted on his face as he greeted those arriving at the same time. The taxi driver looked on ruefully.

The next hour passed uneventfully. Getting to the fares wasn't a problem as he had a map. The problem came when they said where they wanted to go. He had pride and didn't want to look as if it was his first day, that he didn't always know where to go, and had to look up his map or ask. Reactions were mixed. From some it was "nae bother son I'll show you the way". From others it was an incredulous look that a local taxi driver did not know where the Masonic club was. He decided just to admit, 'first day on the job and my mind's gone blank, can you just remind me where that is'. That seemed to be the tactic that drew less disparaging remarks. But he hated looking as if he didn't know what he was doing, especially in front of the type of people he was used to ordering about. His mood darkened as the night wore on, listening to blathering nonsense, and wrestling in the rain with streets that had no logic as to how they numbered their houses.

Then he got a call to Edinburgh Airport to pick up a local company director off the last London flight. He stood in Arrivals but no one responded to his sign. He went back to his car where he could hear an increasingly agitated voice calling for him to answer.

"The guy's going ballistic, he's been waiting 30 minutes, where are you?"

He dashed back in to where he had been told to go, and caught up with a pretty pissed-off looking late forties suit, who wasted no time in telling him how crap his taxi company were, how stupid he was, and who looked as if the BA miniature trolley on the flight had taken a severe hit.

It's not terribly pleasant being in a car with someone who has taken a right royal huff with you, but as his passenger spent the entire 45 minutes on the phone, cajoling, bullying, organising, and loudly pontificating to his unfortunate minions still working at this late hour, at least there was no awkward silence. He dropped him off at home, receiving barely a grunt or thank you, almost as if the driver wasn't a human being at all, but a mechanical extension of the car. "Thank you too" he mouths quietly and sarcastically as the suit stomps up the path, anxious wife peeking through the curtains, probably scared that the dinner was ruined and it would be her fault. It was a scene strangely familiar.

He began to learn that appearances can be deceptive. Some folks might talk nonsense but at least they have humanity and soul. Some might be half cut but they don't treat him like a piece of shit on a shoe. Some might be from a run down area but they are off to start night shift for a pittance rather than draw the dole. Some might look older than they are, but only because they have had the type of life he could never survive.

Deep down however, his first shift's experience only served to remind him of how he'd once had it all, and how far he had fallen, when the daily nightcap became a bottle. And the tears came, not loud crying just silent sobbing, but tears for what he once had, what he became, and the pit into which he dropped.

By now the rain was pouring heavily. He was still quietly sobbing but there were no windscreen wipers to clear his eyes. It must have taken a few seconds but everything was so vivid. He didn't see the drunk lurching off the pavement until the last second. The brakes screeched, the wheels veered sharply right, as he thought bugger this, putting up with crap all night and now I'm killing someone. How can you think all that in a micro second? Contact was just avoided. He jumped out berating the sad looking apology for a human being scrabbling in the gutter - mouthing obscenities at no one and nothing in particular. He gave him a mouthful of his own and roared off. And then it hit him. Had he not also scrabbled around in his own gutter? He stopped the car, and for the third time tonight thought 'I used to be you'. And he also remembered the stranger's kindness rescuing him from that gutter and starting his journey back. The tears dried, he smiled - and turned back.

The Minotaur

by Ian Ellis

Time and the company
have taken my life.
When I joined I was excited,
all posh I was dressed.
My great grandmother died,
when she was eighty-five,
I started to die the day I joined.
I got stuck in the labyrinth.
We have no Theseus
or Ariande,
So I asked my friend
the boss,
for a reprieve,
he just laughed.
He became death,
a destroyer of worlds.
I did not know
his loyalty was to the company.

It Cannot Be Crushed

by Jim Kean

In the midst of the slum lies a diamond
Sparkling defiance of despair
From atrocity comes bravery
Piercing the mask evil wears
Selfish acts are surpassed by the selfless
About whom we never get to hear
They don't make news

From the depths of the pit rise heroes
Clawing their way to the sun
Around needles and squalor angels tread
Who don't judge, give up, or run
Despite all we contrive to break it with
Great human spirit remains
It cannot be crushed.

The Phone Call
by Paul Green

While Jeffrey slept the sun swung across the sky on its arch by almost
imperceptible degrees, and gradually slipped beneath the horizon as
nightfall impatiently slunk in under a dark blanket. In response the lamps in
the street outside flickered on, providing isolated beacons of light that
wavered against the oppressive gloom besieging them.

Jeffrey stirred slightly in his sleep, a judder running the length of his body
as darkness invaded the room around him, inking all colour from his
surroundings. The fire just beyond his outstretched feet had dwindled down
to a heap of dulling embers that cast ownerless, dancing shadows across the
walls. From shelves in a cabinet nearby ornate buffalo, otters and old men
stared on lifelessly. All was still, all was silent.

A thump from upstairs punctuated the quiet suddenly. Jeffrey's eyes
sprung open to find the afternoon long gone and another darkness replacing
the one he had just emerged from. While every other muscle in his body
became as taut as tension line his eyes roved frantically in their sockets
travelling over the veined ceiling above. He held his breath, awaiting a repeat
of the sound, but heard only the clunk of the grandfather clock in the
hallway, announcing the passing seconds with the same sense of foreboding
that was already gripping him possessively.

He dared a glance through the gap in the doorframe, catching sight of the
red phone on its cradle in the hallway. How quickly could he reach it? Would
it bring about a flurry of activity from above that would culminate in a
frantic scream for help down the receiver? At the very thought the blood
began to drain from his whitening face. Clunk the clock said from beyond
the room. Clunk it repeated a second later. Clunk.

As the passing seconds swelled to minutes and with only a deafening silence for company, the thought occurred to Jeffrey for a heartbeat to call out, but the apprehension of being answered stayed his tongue. Instead he simply waited while the last glowing cinders of the fire faded to charcoal. Complete darkness then settled into the room

It took the better part of half an hour for his muscles to fully loosen and rationality to slowly reassert itself in his mind, reassuring him that there were numerous explanations for the thump, the most likely of which was an open window slamming closed under a breeze, if he had indeed left one open that was.

The longer he sat in the dark the more ridiculous he began to feel, and the more unfounded his fears became. Had his wife still been breathing she would have had something to say about a seventy year old man jumping in his own home at the slightest sound. Feeling foolish he exhaled loudly and, using the arms of the chair he eased himself to his feet, the very movement granting him confidence. From where he stood he could see across the road to the adjacent street, where a row of houses were brightly lit from behind closed curtains. Graham at number thirty four looked to have visitors tonight if the line of cars parked outside his house were any indication. Jeffrey sighed and turned from the window, his stomach growling a complaint to which it received a reassuring pat.

With a limping gait he left the room, flicking on the light switch behind him before stepping out into the hallway. He cast an accusatory glance up towards the murk of the landing then shuffled down the hall, past the phone and the grandfather clock, its face reading eleven twenty five.

As he entered the kitchen his hand instinctively found the light switch and tapped it on. At once the room was flooded with brightness, showing his reflection mirroring him in the blackly framed window as he crossed the room to the fridge. There he pulled free a wedge of cheese, which he unwrapped and began slicing into layers before arranging them between two slices of bread from a nearby loaf. No sooner had he done this though, when the phone abruptly rang out from the hallway. He turned from the kitchen worktop and dumbly stood listening to its urgent tone for a moment. He considered not answering it. This was the time of night that usually heralded bad news. The phone continued to ring though, insistently until it spurred him to hobble out of the kitchen and back into the long hallway, mentally checked off relatives against the likelihood of them calling him at this time of night. Even as he pulled the red telephone free of its cradle he could not think of a single name. He raised the phone to his right ear.

"Hello?" he asked apprehensively.

"Hi Jeffrey" came the cheerful voice of his agent.

"Hello Gerry."

A sound of slurping complemented the image Jeffrey had of him in his mind, a cigarette in one hand and a mug of coffee in the other.

"Just a quick call Jeffrey regarding the latest short you gave us last week. The Phone Call?"

"What did you think of it?" Jeffrey asked, hopefully.

"I loved it. It's your best yet. I think we could have it in print by October."

"Music to my ears Gerry. There's always bills needing paid."

"Well, you keep writing the stories and we'll carry on writing the cheques." Jeffrey forced a laugh.

"I'll call you later in the week to let you know how we're getting on," Gerry told him.

"Cheers."

"Speak to you then. Cheers."

The line clicked and left a dull tone in Jeffrey's ear. He replaced the phone on its cradle and then, rubbing his hands together he wandered back into the kitchen, watching his reflection follow him to the bunker. Absent-mindedly he picked up the sandwich and raised it to his mouth while staring into the impenetrable darkness beyond the window, completely unaware of the peculiar shaped bite already taken out of it.

Dear Mum
by Rebecca Dadge

Dear Mum

You were sleeping when Emma and I arrived at the hospital today. What is it about hospital beds that make people look instantly vulnerable? My stomach lurched at the sight of you, my Amazon Woman of a Mother looking, Oh My God, just like anybody else. The nurse tells us to wait in the Family Room where the consultant will come and talk to us.

This particular room is obviously a converted cupboard that someone has tried to transform into a friendly and cosy environment, with heartbreakingly little effect. The room is long and narrow, wallpapered in horrible pastel shades with a border around it, positioned halfway up the wall. There are bland pictures of trees and landscapes on the wall picked to fit in with the colour scheme is seems, rather than any artistic merit. Two chairs are placed at the far end of the room and one chair facing toward them next to the door. The chair-to-door dynamic suggests the careful placing of furniture to avoid those being told bad news bolting from the room. I can imagine the consultant just putting out his leg for us to do a prat fall in an attempt to avoid hearing the worst.

This reminds me of that woman I used to work with who received a phone call early one morning at work. I answered the phone and handed her the receiver and told her it was her brother. She looked immediately afraid – it turned out they had not spoken for years. She spoke into the phone 'what is it Kenny?' and then a few moments passed and she shouted 'dinnae be telling me that Kenny. Oh God, dinnae be telling me that' as her brother broke the news that her mother had died that morning. As though taking the words back would change the facts.

Anyway, Emma and I peer reluctantly into the Family Room. Despite your best efforts there's no doubt we've seen way too many TV dramas – basically we know this for a fact; never in the history of TV or movie dramas does anybody leave a Family Room feeling better than when they went in and in fact, they usually feel much, much worse. We look at each other, then back into the room, then back at each other – neither of use making a move to step inside. We start to giggle because we know we are both thinking the same thing. Maybe if we didn't go in the Family Room and chose instead to pack your belongings, take you home, life could go on as usual. It was certainly a plan worth consideration.

Part of me thinks it would somehow be more honest if they had left the cupboard intact. It was shaping up to be a shitty day anyway and I briefly imagine having to squeeze by shelves full of freshly ironed linen and stepping over a linoleum buffer; Emma and I huddled into the end, one of us puffing guilty on a cursed cigarette, the hateful root of all our troubles, opening a small window, caked with many years of peeling paint in order to blow smoke out of the window and not set off any alarms.

We sit in the room and the consultant comes in. He explains that you were due for a biopsy that morning anyway and with the fits you'd been having they were giving you a brain scan. They were looking for lung cancer with a possibly secondary cancer in the brain. I surprise myself by asking a lot of calm and intelligent questions. What was the likelihood? Had he seen this sort of thing before? Blah, blah, blah I went. The consultant is quiet and serious but like many of his profession, somewhat hesitant and uncomfortable when talking to human beings – that is, until I ask him what he expects to find. Then something shifts significantly, he becomes more confident, his whole body language changes from awkward professional to competent diagnostic, he leans back, shoulders slackening as he relaxes – I have inadvertently wandered into his Area of Expertise. As soon as my brain registers this, I want to put my hand up and say 'Stop! Stop! I didn't mean to ask a good, articulate question! I take it back!' or put my fingers in my ears and hum loudly until he stops but it's too late for that, the consultant is on a roll. He assures us he has seen this many times before and, basically, if it turns out not to be lung cancer with a secondary brain cancer he'll be very surprised. His assuredness is devastating. He leaves the room to check on something leaving us sitting in stunned silence. 'Oh my God' I say to my sister 'this is serious. I mean this is serious'. My sister wipes tears from her face. The consultant comes back in the room and is momentarily taken aback that the two poised and calm people he left a few minutes beforehand are weeping wrecks, shadows of their former selves.

Haiku
by Alan MacFarlane

A day-dreaming girl
flicks droplets from her jacket
at a wet bus stop

A Dare Too Far
by Derenz

With my niece I escape to uncharted
slopes. I challenge her to greater dares.
She slips. A crane driver hollers. My
wheelchair slews, bumps and bounces. I
scream as hidden steps pitch me out,
buckle my wheels.

Mum rages. Blames and bars my niece.
Imprisoned at home, I cry alone.

The Fire Fighter
by Abid Rasul

Lee sat there watching the forensics trying to make head or tail of the situation. He was the only person who could have seen what had happened and not a blink did he miss.

"Paralysed" the doctors had said. "Paralysed for life unless he wants to move. Show him some happy memories and make him want to live them again."

Lee was a hefty fire fighter, the strongest and bravest in the force. He would not waste a second of his time on the job, not even to locate his axe. Instead, if the need arose he would tear away doors with his bare hands.

It was a Saturday, Lee's day off. It went by like any other, until night spread its blanket over the sky. Lee noticed an odour lingering in the background. His mind was telling him it was a smell he was well acquainted with but he just could not place it. Five minutes went by, ten minutes went by, but still the same problem.

"My baby! My baby!" the neighbour's cry made everything slot into place. How could he not recognise the smell of smoke? "Irresponsible" he thought to himself. "Negligent and foolish." Now he had to make the situation right.

He burst through the door, not waiting for the fire brigade to arrive. He crawled through the flames like a beast in search for prey. Room by room he went, not wanting to miss what he was in search of. He could feel the scorching flames burning away the hair on his arms and legs and his skin began to crisp. Then as he squinted through the dense smoke he saw the boy. There he was, cornered by the flames creeping closer and closer. Lee knew he had to get to him and fought his way through the battling fire. He reached the child and sheltered him with his own body.

He woke in hospital bandaged from head to toe. His daughter was there talking to the doctor. "The boy, Stephen, is fine just a few minor burns." he overheard the doctor say. "As for your father; all his nerve endings have burnt away. He has lost his sense of touch and his body is paralysed. You will have to help him pull out of it."

Every morning since then, before going to work, she would take him out to the garden and leave him under the shade of their gazebo facing the neighbour's garden. She hoped that seeing Stephen growing up would make him want to live his life again.

There he was, the same routine everyday, watching his neighbours spoil their son. They would give him anything he asked for. "God gave him to us twice" they would say if anyone ever questioned them. "Wouldn't you spoil your children if the same happened to them?" By the age of seven he began answering them back. By nine he was uncontrollable.

Stephen noticed Lee's eyes following him around. It started with him sticking his tongue out at Lee and making funny faces. But with time respect dies and Stephen was too young to know what Lee had done for him. "What y' lookin' at, y' auld git!" was a warning that he was going to do something obscene. One of Stephen's favourites was to walk into Lee's garden and moony him a few inches from his face. "Who will know?" Stephen would think to himself. "Isn't as if he can talk or move." Then the peashooter and paper pellets started and then the plastic dart gun. By this time Lee wished his emotions had died along with his sense of touch.

Stephen's mum bought him a ball. He kicked the ball and it went into Lee's garden. Stephen went to fetch the ball. After picking it up he thought he would have a laugh. "Hey, auld man, see if y' can head the ba'." He threw it lightly at first and it rebounded off Lee's head. Then he threw it with a bit more force, and harder and harder still. Soon he was going for the title 'fastest bowler in the world'. "Damn!" He bowled a wide and right into the back of the gazebo it went.

"...make him want to move." The doctor's words rang in Lee's ears. Stephen was behind him in the gazebo picking up his ball. Lee's fingers began to twitch. His muscles began to spasm and his body began to shake. Stephen, terrified, backed away into the corner. "Are you okay, Lee? What's happening to you, Lee? Relax, Lee. I'll go and call the doctor, Lee." There was no way out. Lee blocked the only exit, and he didn't want to even go close to him.

Lee stretched out one leg and then the next. He pushed himself up and stood there. Turning his head he looked at Stephen. There he was, now seven years down the line. The same fear in his eyes as Lee had seen during the fire.

Stephen saw this burnt creature staring at him. No hair, not even an eyebrow or an eyelash. "Run! Run!" he told himself, but his legs refused to cooperate.

Lee walked towards him and reached out to him. He placed his hand on his head and ran his palm down his cheek. His hand paused just below the chin. His fingers clasped the throat and his grip began to tighten. Stephen could no longer breathe. Lee lifted him off the ground. Then together with his other hand, in one swift move, he broke his neck. He swung the boy back over into his back yard.

One of the forensics spotted the ball in the back of the gazebo. He walked over to Lee and stared into his eyes. He took the top off his pen and stabbed Lee in the thigh. Apart from the light sound of breathing there was no sign of life. He shook his head and walked away mumbling, "I know he knows what happened."

Once Upon A Time
by Stefano Turato

"Dad, why can't we see them?"

"Darling, if you see one, it'll turn to stone."

"But it's not fair, I want to see one and take it home with me. I promise I'll look after it."

"I'm sure you would but you can't take it home anyway. Faeries live in the woods because that's their home. If you start taking the little folk from their home the rest of their friends and family will come after you."

"Why?"

"Because they would be angry."

"Why? I would take it on an adventure to see all of my friends. It would have a lovely time."

"Well, maybe your idea of fun is not their idea of fun."

"How do you know that?"

"I don't know for certain, I'm just saying that it could be."

"You shouldn't say things like that if you don't mean it?"

"It's not that I don't mean it, I'm just trying to explain to you that sometimes other people or other things in life may not like the things that you like. We are all different."

"Miss Ferguson said that we are all the same and that we are not different and we shouldn't treat people differently."

"Your teacher is right darling. We are all the same, no matter what colour, or size or shape and of course we should treat each other the same."

"But that is what I'm saying – I do want to treat the faeries the same as me."

"That's different."

"Why?"

"Because they are little and they belong in the woods."

"But you shouldn't treat them differently because they are smaller or because they live in a different place."

"No, you shouldn't. What I mean is we should treat them with consideration."

"Does that mean that we should treat others differently and not with consideration?

"No that's not what I mean. What I am trying to say is that we should treat each other the same and because faeries are special we should treat them with consideration and respect how they live and what they want to do."

"That's fine. But what about the faerie children?"

"We should treat them the same and respect their wishes also."

"What is respect?"

"Respect? It means consideration!"

"What is consideration?"

"Consideration means that we should think about the wishes of others."

"So, the faerie children have got respect but normal children haven't, is that right?"

"No! That's not correct. What makes you say that?"

"Well, sometimes when I want to do something, you say 'I can't', or, 'I don't care what you want, you're not getting it."

"That's only when you are naughty or if you have asked for something you shouldn't have, like when you ask for sweeties at bedtime."

"But if you had respect, you wouldn't say those things."

"Respect is earned."

"What is earned?"

"Deserved!"

"What is deserved?"

"It is when you are due something, like, say, if you tidy your room, you get sweeties."

"So if I tidy my room at bedtime will I get a sweetie at bedtime?"

"No! You don't get sweeties at bedtime."

"But you should give me sweeties if I have tidied my room."

"Not at bedtime. That's different!"

"Why is it always different?"

"Look! You asked me about respect. Well, children need to earn respect, and asking me all these ridiculous questions will not earn my respect. Doing as you are told and behaving will earn my respect."

"You are not being very considerate are you?"

"Can we change the subject?"

"I don't want to change anything except you dad. You are not fair. I only wanted to see a faerie."

"If you don't stop speaking you'll never see one. They like the silence!"

"Okay dad, I'll be quiet so I can earn your respect."

"Thank the Lord…

… Wonders will never cease…

…maybe we can continue our walk through the woods and maybe we shall see a faerie…

… darling?

Darling… are you ok?…

… Oh I get it; I'm going to get the silent treatment… in that case you won't be able to ask any questions… nor will you be able to shout for joy when you see a faerie… and you won't be able to tell mummy about what you have seen… and, oh look, what's that moving in that bush over there?"

"Where, daddy, where?"

"Didn't last long did it, the silent treatment?"

"Oh daddy, that's mean, you mean old thingy. You tricked me!"

"No I didn't, there is something in that bush."

"What is it?"

"I don't know. I can only see what you can see!"

"There's no need to be horrible, I'm only asking."

"Listen! If we are too noisy they'll never come out."

"What will never come out?"

"I don't know, I'm saying that whoever, or whatever is in that bush, will not come out because it'll be too bloody frightened with all the noise."

"Don't say bloody, it's naughty."

"Stop! Just be quiet, please, please."

"No!"

"Darling! Any more of this behaviour and we'll go home."

"Good! I don't want to stay here anyway."

"You'll wait until I'm ready."

"Why? Is it because you want to see the faeries too?"

"Don't be daft, there's no such thing as, uhm… I mean of course not, well, yes, I do actually; yes I want to see the faeries. We'll both watch that bush to see what comes out."

"Why don't we get a bit closer dad, come on?"

"If we get too close it'll run away. It's probably just a squirrel anyway."

"I want to see it before it runs away forever, and it'll be all your fault."

"Come back here!"

"Dad, look?"

"What is it?"

"Come and see."

"Has it gone? What was it? A bird or a rabbit or something?"

"No dad, I think it was a faerie."

"Don't be silly, it couldn't have been. It would have turned to stone. Remember?

"Dad, it's a tiny doorway with a tiny handle, and look inside dad. There are tiny steps going down."

A Wee Morality Tale
by Mike Mitchell

Jan decided, before he kicked away the shabby Bristol Rovers duvet, that he would dog school today. Fourth Year maths and English before the dinner break helped his decision. Instinctively, he knew that his teachers would heave a silent sigh of gratitude.

An only child, he was 'on trust' with his mum, who, as a local postie, started work at five o' clock every morning bar Sunday. She wouldn't be home till nearly noon and Jan planned to be gone by then. He'd take his satchel with him and hide it somewhere till coming home time, a ploy that usually worked. Comfortable in his deceit, the teenager staggered into his baggies and Golas and went through to the small kitchen.

A slice of yesterday's pepperoni pizza was breakfast, along with a hasty mouthful of flat lemonade. Meanwhile Jan finished dressing. A Black Sabbath tee-shirt and an outsize black hoodie completed his ensemble. One more thing to do before he could hit the street; Jan rifled through every pocket, handbag and drawer in the flat and came up with one pound and sixty-two pence, enough to buy a snack later. He pulled the front door firmly after him, checking that he had double-locked it. Can't be too careful, he thought, too many bloody thieves about. Bouncing down the four flights of concrete stairs to the untidy street, he was on his way.

It was Thursday, pension day, and old people were out in droves at the local shopping centre. Jan dodged through the minefield of spindly legs, zimmers and walking sticks, ignoring comments about him not being in school. He headed towards a new mall in busier part of town, somewhere where he wasn't known, where he could blend in. It wouldn't do to be spotted by a teacher or worse, a policeman, who might think he was some sort of cheap, petty criminal. Twenty minutes later, he was in downtown Bristol. The pavements were flooded with people going about the business of life. Jan relaxed.

He checked the clock outside Debenham's, nearly half eleven, time for a bite. A tiny corner café in a quiet part of the mall attracted him. In he went. He could afford it, he found, checking the menu on the counter.

"Give us an onion pastie," he told the shop-girl.

"One pound twenty," she answered automatically, shovelling one into a paper bag and sliding it over the counter top with one hand, while the other snatched his cash, quick as a serpent's tongue.

Two silver-haired 'old dears' sitting at the nearest table, sipping hot tea from thin Styrofoam cups, tutted to each other in disgust.

"What a pity they don't teach 'em manners these days, eh, Gert?"

"Har! A right bleedin pity, Augustine."

Jan threw them a withering stare as he turned to leave. Then added,

"Don't diss me, you old crones! What 'ave your lot done for me, eh? A drain on the fucken economy, you are. Oughta bring in yuffenasia. Sort you out, that would,"

Their jaws dropped, scalding tea dribbled between their angry, shaking fingers, burning them. One cup fell splat on the floor, wetting their shoes, making them both do a jig while still sitting.

"Oi! Watch out!" shouted the shop girl. "I'll have to clean up the mess, you know."

Jan ran, a wide smile fixed on his face.

He stopped nearby and sat on a wooden bench next to some miniature palm trees where he attacked the crumbly pastie, wolfing it down in three mouthfuls. Wiping the grease from his lips on a sleeve, he felt the girl from the shop suddenly sit down beside him.

" 'ello," spluttered Jan, firing crumbs everywhere.

" 'ello yerself," she answered.

"Wash yer name then?"

"Patty. What's yourn."

"Jan."

She pulled a can of juice from a coat pocket.

"Want some?"

"D'you nick it?"

"Maybe."

He gave her his best doubtful stare and she drew the can back, making it look as if she was keeping it.

" Yeh, awright then, give it 'ere."

He wrenched off the tab and drank, emitting a belch loud enough to draw looks of disgust from passers by. Patty laughed and instantly Jan lost his heart. When she added, "Them two ol' bags went potty when you said that yuffernasia thing," Jan guffawed, unable to stop the blush spreading to the top of his face. He wiped juice from his chin on his sleeve. He knew he was staring at the girl but he didn't care.

Behind them, two glaziers were scrutinising an enormous sheet of plate-glass that had just been fitted into a shop front, its predecessor having fallen victim to some louts the previous evening. They laboriously hoisted their tool bags and walked towards the entrance.

"Pity we ran out of putty, Pete," said Howard, the gaffer.

"I'll come round this afternoon an' do her proper. Okay?"

"Yeh, Pete, that'll do nice."

Jan and Patty, finished with their juice, were holding hands and talking about football. He was a Rovers fan, whereas he loved City. They were oblivious to others walking passed, might have been on their own desert island. They were interrupted by the piercing scream of tortured glass behind them. Both turned as one and froze to see the huge, puttyless plate of heavy glass reach over them, like a see-through angel of death. Their reflections showed only their terrified and uncomprehending faces staring back.

Jan's mum, home from delivering the mail, sat wearily on the battered settee, savouring her cup of coffee. She had checked her son's bedroom when she came in and noticed that his satchel was gone. Good, she thought, maybe he's learning. She clicked the teevee remote and was in time to watch some social commentary on the damage to society caused by children who wouldn't attend school.

"I'll do him some spag bol for his tea," she droned, her brain comfortingly slipping into neutral.

Abracadabra S. J. Peploe
by James Watters McKean

Smoke whirls in the glittering light of your alchemy studio.
There and then, here and now, you summon optimism, from colour.
Violet velvet ribbons roll through and the granite green hills,
Insistent, against a calm azure sea and the relentless Scots pessimism.

Your visions framed in a vacuum of time; offer light and hope,
the simple pleasures of a well-lived Scottish life,
evoking strong black coffee in a bright silver pot.
Conveyed through explosive-yellow-dynamite-sunlight, blasted onto canvas.

Conjuring life and breathing elegance into women long dead.
With a head full of midnight blue, scarlet and knowing.
Your ghost white phantoms are continually escaping from the dark
to the light.
These illusions, bold and certain, hint at the nationality of god;
and I understand, in painting, as in poetry, colour is more important than
line.

Ryan
by Paul Green

The sun. The sun is forever. Unequivocal, inevitable. A hot white portal, unaffected by the great blue expanse and fluffy cotton monoliths that share its realm. Eroder of shadows, nullifier of night-terrors, now reduced to four neon strips of red between four fingers. Now wide, bright shafts, now bands of red.

Smiling, Ryan lets his arms fall loosely to his sides and marches along the dirt path, stabbing his feet in clouds of dust that linger in the busy air. A bumble bee drones past drunkenly, high on pollen and blossom and on a whim Ryan follows under an overhanging canopy of trees, mimicking its warm, preoccupied buzz between clenched teeth and over a vibrating tongue.

Search beam shafts of light burst through the ceiling foliage, dappling the dry dirt floor but the bumblebee's navigation controls are alive to the danger and it skirts the beams with lazy, looping arcs. Ryan follows its lead, pulling down his visor and thumbing the invisible yoke from side to side, guiding his fuzzy craft in a similar manner.

To his right Bumblebee One tapers off to refuel in the centre of a flower pod leaving Ryan alone in the long, green tunnel, save for the occasional pocket of midge fighters agitating the air ahead. Having no wish for any confrontation today he swoops in low and lands near some jettisoned canisters.

With a hiss Bumblebee Two's glass casing opens up allowing Captain Ryan to leap from the craft down to the dusty terrain below. There, he adjusts his wrist calibrator to the local atmosphere, and takes in the strong smell of vegetation before setting off on an exploratory sweep of the area, starting with an investigation of the metal canisters by the edge of the jungle.

'Sweetheart Stout' the markings along the rim of one container state, a logo repeated on each of the four others, along with adorned images of the same woman who appears to be promoting the contents, most probably liquid fuel. Captain Ryan pulls free his neutraliser and sets off in search of the ship as Bumblebee One buzzes overhead providing aerial cover. Surely it could not have gotten far after dumping its fuel canisters he thought. Indeed, further evidence of wreckage lay strewn ahead in the form of items of clothing, shed, no doubt, as a result of the unfamiliar climate the crew would have encountered upon landing.

Suddenly, voices, but from which direction he could not tell. Frantically he turns on the spot searching for cover, noticing as he does so two long, dark shadows stretching across the path in a shaft of light. He had been compromised! A rustling sound and the parting of some bushes up ahead preceded the appearance of two humanoids on the path, one male and the other female. They appear startled for a fraction of a second as they spot him but then continued towards him undeterred. As casually as he can he slings his neutraliser over one shoulder and saunters past them, countering their smiles with barely concealed suspicion. He watches his right foot follow his left for twenty paces then turns to see the humans recede into the distance until a line of trees and bushes along the path swallows them from sight.

After a hundred yards or so the path opens up under the blue and brightness of the sky, replacing the claustrophobic flora of the trees with endless fields of golden flowers that seem to harness the light of the sun, returning its rays from their upturned petals. Captain Ryan can feel his eyes narrow to arrow slits as he takes in the rolling hillsides that appear to be stained as if by a vast ochre brush. Strange world.

Beep Beep his wrist calibrator sounds off, alerting him to his dwindling air vac supply. The meter level shows the red bar to be just shy of eight units, allowing for another fifteen clicks of exploration, time enough for a survey of the surrounding lands before returning to Bumblebee Two for a fresh gulp. Then again, he thought, it was chicken nuggets for tea tonight at base camp. Exploration could wait another day, and with that decided he set off for Bumblebee Two, kicking up dust that was still swirling in the air long after he had left the path for the pavement of the main street.

Skating On Gartmorn Dam

by Jane M Spence

We trudged along as bairns
Lookin fur some fun:
The Dam was a guy lang way off
An' we had tae foot it, everyone
Nae big cars in thae days
But companionship was great
An' so the venue fur the day
Wis a place whereon tae skate.

There wis the Delph at Tullibody
But it wis kind o' sma
Sae the place we loved the maist
Wis Gartmorn Dam or naw;
Nae matter if Jack Frost
Nipped oor hands an' taes
The thocht o' what awaited us
Gave us unco Grace.

There wis Elsie an' Lizzie
There wis Betty an' me
No a skate amongst us
But we were gaun tae see
The lucky an' the plucky,
The lads aboot the place;
Oor presence there wid cheer them on
As they glided ower the ice.

They found their wae fae Queen Street,
An Erskine Street as well
Fae Hill Street an' Greenfield Street
I think ye'll mind them well,
No forgetting Cousins Buildings
Nor Tullibody Road
Izaat Street, Jamaica Street,
A mixed an' happy brood.

Aye, they were the days
When we enjoyed good fun;
Oor 'peevers' an' oor 'girders'
When Schule fur the day wis done;
There wis 'Rally O' an 'Kick the Can'
An' concerts roon the back
When we sang 'Hulikadoo'
Or 'Madam will you walk?'

Many hiv noo left us
An' crossed the Great Divide;
Some laid doon there lives fur us
We remember them wi' pride;
Its nice tae ken midst the throng
O' folks we daily meet
There are those who belong tae the Old Brigade
An' share their memories sweet.

Death Is A Release
by Tricia Golledge

Ah look at ye Tam. Look at you lying there in your patched cardi. A shrunken deid auld man. Oh I shouldn't giggle but you can't do anyone any harm now can you? The boys wanted to bury you in your suit, but I was adamant. It never really was you, anyway, eh? You were much happier in that scabby thing.

They are both here, Tam, the Boys. They are waiting outside, trying to be brave. It's been nice having them around, been too many years since they were both in the house together. They still bicker all the time.

The wee boy from the Co-operative was nice. But it's bad enough being an undertaker without having to dress them like one eh? Christ, Tam you would have laughed. He even had a black coat on. But, see, you look well now, eh? They've done a nice job. I always said you looked better with your teeth in. Willie didnae think I was capable of choosing the coffin. You know they had a brochure! A brochure of coffins! Can you imagine? If it had been up to Willie you'd have been in a cardboard one, but that was the same price as the plywood. This mid-oak turned out better than I thought. Willie choked because it was near a thousand pounds. More than you deserve isn't it and I bet is pissing you off.

Oh here, guess who popped in just after the undertaker – Nora Douglas. Remember Nora Green married oan tae Bertie Douglas, the electrician? Dae ye ken what she had the cheek to say to me?

"I've just come to offer my condolences"

Can you believe it? That's something you say to some wifey you nod to in the passing. No someone who has kent ye for thirty odd year. Of all the insincere clichés, honestly. She should be the last person coming out with that to me. I was so angry I almost punched her. Well I roared at her

"Condolences! My man's fucking deid!" I did, that was the actual words. The boys thought I had went off ma heid. But no me. I was just so angry. Bet you never thought you'd see the day eh, Tam? Ah well neither did Nora Douglas.

"Oh, Nellie," she said "I'm only paying my respects". Her and her pan loaf accent.

Anyway I let rip tae Nora. Because after all, she, of all people, knew that she should be congratulating me not giving me her condolences.

I know I used to moan about her cadging shillings for the meter and her snotty, dirty bairns who were aye round tae play with the boys at dinner or tea time. You must remember that they were good neighbours, tae? Well you probably won't remember but it was Nora that found me after that time I told you I was pregnant again. She made sure the boys were out of the way, she cleaned up the blood, and she made sure you didn't come home till I'd recovered a little. It was even Nora that started the rumour about me falling off the sink, to protect us – no to protect you, from the gossip. She knew only too well what ye were like. Yet she still went with you didn't she?

I wasn't as stupid as you made me out to be you know. I knew about the money. I asked Shuggy McGlynn what your wages were, so I knew that you'd gave her a pound or two. And for what Tam? Because it flattered your vanity that you were calling the shots. No some sad git that traipsed home on a Friday and handed the wage packet to the little woman. No you'd rather your bairns went hungry so you could sneak up the close wie some cheap slattern for a shag. Several times tae, eh Tam?

I wisnae the only yin that knew. Did you never wonder why Bertie and Nora moved away quick? Well you were always a self obsessed bastard. Your death's done me the world of good I'm swearing a lot now.

The boys were a bit shocked. I even felt a bit sorry for Willie, only for a minute though. He looked like he was going to greet.

"Ma Dad wisnae a bad man. I dinae want to hear you talking about him like that"

And for a second I could see you there, smirking, all of you standing against me, and looking at me as if I was senile. I'm not having it, so I kicked the lot of them out.

"Bugger off" I roared at the boys

They've been back, just to finalise the arrangements, they're outside now, they want to see you and the parlour's closing soon. Seeing them sitting side by side you wouldn't take them as brothers would ye? You always laughed at the differences, always joked about Willie being the double spit of you, even down tae the tight-fistedness and the temper. Johnnie, yer golden boy, he's racked with guilt because he hadn't been hame so often. I've tried to tell him he's not to go down that road. You were such a nasty, cantankerous bastard the last few months, its no wonder he didn't want to put up with yer moaning and criticising. Not when he didn't need to. Johnnie was only mine, Tam. He's nothing to do with you. How could a twisted, selfish oaf like you have produced that kind, even tempered boy? He's more like his father, the one man who'd been gentle and kind to me, for a while anyway. Did that shock you?

Well you'll have plenty of time to think it over where you're going. So I'll say cheerio, Tam. I can hear the little undertaker saying it's always worse with a sudden death. But we ken it wisnae that sudden, eh Tam. It had been coming for a while – for forty-seven years.

Increasing Force 9, Easing Later

by JB Steel

(v. Tennyson, 'The Lotos Eaters')

wind and wave and oar
  winD and waVe and oaroar
   wiND and waVE and oaroaroar
    wIND and wAVE oaroaroaroaroar
     WINDWAVE WINDWAVE oaroaroaroaroaroar
    WINd and WAVe oaroaroaroaroar
   WInd and WAve and oaroaroar
  Wind and wAve and oaroar
wind and wave and oar

In The Quiet Of The Night

by Leela Sanchdev

Just-before the Sun sank deep
Behind the flamed-orange sky,
And the shadows melted
Into the tranquillity of the dusk,
The seeping silence
Lulled the mahogany trees;
Just after the evening meal,
On chipped enamel plates, vanished
Crumb at a time, held with tiny fingers
And the quivering yellow of the wick
In the kerosene lamp flickered to ebony black;
Then in the quiet of the time,
Every hand pulled up blanket, chin-deep,
Eye lids closed tight, fists clenched hard;
A sweep of air traced their facial features,
Wiping away frowns on their faces.

Where Do I Start?
by Julie Rose Clark

Where did I start?
TRULY?
Was it in Darlington
In 1969?
Was it 9 months before?
God knows where.

Where do I start now?
Ask Jesus Christ to
reveal himself to you.
He will not ask
anything of you.
He has already accepted you.

Where do I find this peace?
I know He will help me.
I'm glad I am talking about it.
I'm glad I am finally asking.
I'm glad I am at long last broken.
This opportunity not to be missed

nor walked by –
for I walked past deaf and unwilling
for too many years
refusing to listen
and suiting only myself
MYSELF.

Finnegan's Boots
by Stefano Turato

"To whom do these boots belong?" enquired the old lady, holding up a pair of boots in one hand whilst pushing up her glasses with the other. But the regulars of Finnegan's Fake were busy chatting and enjoying their drinks to hear her fragile tones above the din. She hoisted her stiff leg up on to a chair and pulled herself up on to a table to be seen. She again held up the boots and the pub went quiet and stared. Then she tried again.

"To whom do these boots belong? I found them outside by the door, only it's about to rain and I couldn't possibly allow them to get wet through. So I brought them in."

After a long silence, where the dryer in the men's toilets was all that could be heard, came a reply.

"Those boots are special lady. They belong to Finnegan."

Stifled laughter. Then silence. The dryer was all that could be heard again.

"Oh, splendid. It would be an awful waste if they are so special. Would Mr. Finnegan kindly step forward and I can pass them to you."

"He passed away many years ago. The nature of his death is not spoken of here. His boots were retrieved, you know, from the scene, and brought back to his favourite place, here beside his old acquaintances where he drank. We take them from that cabinet over there, where they are kept safe. Then we place them outside as a mark of respect on this special day, to commemorate his passing. Always have done, always will. Unless they get stolen."

"Oh my goodness, I had no idea, I'm ever so sorry."

"No harm done. Nonetheless, we would all appreciate you returning the boots to their rightful place, outside, where you found them. In fact, as you rightly say, so they don't get wet, would you kindly put them in that glass cabinet over there, next to the darts trophy?"

The regulars fought hard to withhold their laughter; however, some lost the fight and sniggered. Not hearing, she stepped down from the table and limped to the cabinet. She opened the glass door.

The sound of the dryer stopped then Fergus Slattery emerged from the loo, dutifully relieved and ready for his next pint. Until he saw an old lady putting a pair of boots into the trophy cabinet whilst the whole pub sat silent and watched with utter amazement.

"Hey, what are you doing with my boots?" shouted Fergus.

The pub erupted into a raucous clamour, unable to control themselves from the grip of a bellyaching laugh. It was utter pandemonium. Even Fergus saw the joke and joined in. But the old lady didn't laugh. Instead, she got back up on the table and stared, still holding the boots. There she waited. And when the light from the naked bulb above her head revealed a tear trailing down her cheek the laughter stopped. She carefully lowered herself from her perch and slowly shuffled her way out of the pub door, still clutching the boots. The door swung shut and the old lady was gone. The pub remained silent. Nobody spoke and shamed faces dropped.

The silence eventually broke after a few minutes as the door opened once again. The regulars looked up, perhaps hoping for a chance to redeem themselves. Four sombre looking men walked in, all dressed in black. Surprised by the silence and a little conscious that the whole pub was looking at them, they stopped and looked around. The regulars looked away and they continued their procession towards the bar. The tall man spoke with a deep, guttural voice, filled with sadness.

"Four whiskies, please!" and he placed a fifty pound note on the bar.

Without answering the barman reached for the glasses and placed them on the bar. Then he disappeared through a door into the back room. He was gone for a minute and returned with a new bottle of Grouse. He twisted off the cap and gently poured the four men their drinks without spilling a drop. The tall man passed his shorter acquaintances their glasses, one by one. He raised his glass and the others followed.

The regulars watched, still silent, still shamed, but intrigued by the unfolding drama.

"To Mam" cried the tall man. "To Mam" his brothers replied.

They threw their whiskies to the back of their throats and slammed their empty glasses back down onto the bar.

"Four whiskies, please!" said the tall man once again, but it was a weaker sound this time, more of a request to burn away the pain.

Not a sound could be heard above the liquid pouring into the glasses until the tall man turned to the regulars and shouted,

"Speak! Do you not talk here?"

But the shock of the demand made it worse so the barman volunteered a response.

"I'm sorry about your loss, we all are, but we are just a bit confused and somewhat embarrassed by... shall we say events that occurred before you arrived."

"Our mam, it was our mam." Cried the tall man. His brothers looked on with grief. "Her name was Eve, Evelyn MacKenzie. She came here when she was young. Every Friday night for twenty-three years with Dad until he...until we lost him. But that was a long time ago when we were still young, before we moved away. She never came back. We buried her today. We wanted to come and take a look. Pay our respects. She told us many tales, you know, about this place."

"Evelyn MacKenzie?" said the barman slowly shaking his head "can't remember the name."

"It'll be before your time son. She was short, wore specs, and had a limp from a childhood accident."

The pub door swung open. A chill wind filled the pub and shame turned to fear.

'Starry Night' Run:
Ironing Out The Glitches
by JB Steele

the w   a   r p
FAIL: REJECT
the wo   of
FAIL: REJECT
the   o   n   e
FAIL: REJECT
the w   ag   e   r
FAIL: REJECT
the w r   a t   h
FAIL: REJECT
the r   a   ge
FAIL:REJECT
the r   e   al
FAIL: REJECT
th   r   ar   e
FAIL: REJECT
the work of art in the age of mechanical reproduction
PASS
the work of art in the age of mechanical reproduction
PASS
the work of art in the age of mechanical reproduction
PASS

processed, packaged, and ready to go

Inspired By A Visit To Budapest 2006
by Jean Edgar

On Sunday the robin returned
to the city park
breast brushed with the colour of life
and winged courage
to come much too close.

On Monday the militia marched in
to where the robin trembled in trembling trees,
hope and tiny stones crushed
beneath the grinding tank tracks,
and tramping, tramping, tramping.

On Tuesday the sounds of gunshot
riccocheting off walls through shattered skulls
and pools of blood, congealed,
darker than the robin's breast
and thicker than the autumn mists.

On Wednesday a mother vice-like grips
her children's hands
too small to hold or aim a gun
too young to bear the world of hate against them,
the birds in innocence are free
the children in innocence wake screaming.

Unheard Voices - *An Anthology*

On Thursday men in shabby clothes are mustered
then soldiers weary with long days of marshalling
curse the people for being so many, so slow,
so lacking in understanding.

On Friday the silver birch whisper
and sway in rythmic chorus
surround the stable blocks, the chimneys,
the graves fresh dug,
and some million birds migrate for safety
as winter exhales its hoar frost breath.

On Saturday the robin solitary sweeps
along the river bank
amongst the many discarded shoes
like cast off sea shells
still damp with dew and perspiration,
shaped in life but empty in death,
a temporary perch, that's all,
now ghosts wreathe across
the surface waters
and startled, the little bird flies on.

Dancing In The Dark
by Sylvia Tate

Annie swayed gently to the music as Dean Martin sang. An invisible partner
moved with her as she fluttered and flowed, mouthing the words silently to
herself. Her smiling face reflected a secret inner world that I could only
guess at. Wherever her memory had taken her, it looked a lot more fun than
here. As Annie moved towards me I hesitated to interrupt, enjoying the
performance, but then the space between us disappeared and I felt
compelled to speak or turn away.

'I bet you used to go to the dancing' I grinned, suddenly deciding I needed
to ask.

'Aye, me and ma friends are goin' oot tonight. I'll be goin' for the bus soon.
Afterwards ma mammy will be waitin' at the close door, arms folded like
body armour across her chest.

"Get yourself in here. Do you know whit time it is?" she'll say, not really a
question, pokin' me as I walk past and up the stairs.

Ma mammy always thinks we've been up to mischief but we haven't been
doin' any harm, just oot havin' fun. The Barrowland's the best. Do you ever
go there? We could go thigither. The bands are great and the fellas always
give you a dance, then ask to walk you home. We always say aye but only as
far as the road end, 'cos ma mammy would belt me if she saw me wi' a fella.
Me and Mary live up the same close so mammy knows we always come
home thigither, but she disnae' ken aboot the fellas.' Annie laughed at how
she pulled the wool over her mammy's eyes. I wasn't sure about that because
mothers tend to know these things. I thought about the Barrowland in its
heyday.

As I looked at the lined face of the old woman, smelling her decaying
body, I wondered at the life that used to be.

Unheard Voices - An Anthology

'OK, Annie?' the young girl asked as she started to set the tables for dinner, interrupting my thoughts, but barely registering any recognition on Annie's face.

It was hard to imagine that this old body had once been young. Her grey hair was thin, sticking out in spikes, the pink scalp shining through like the skin of a piglet. Curls and waves, perms and hairclips would have been her style for the dancing, hoping to attract a 'fella' by the gloss and shine of her crowning glory, stiff as a board, maybe with sugar paste on to make sure, if there was sugar to spare. The hairdresser who comes to the home every week tries to do her best but it must be difficult when the raw material is colourless, thin and as decaying as the body and mind it reflects. As I was watching Annie lost in the private world of her youth, I imagined what she would have worn to go out. Not the shabby, slightly stained trousers and jumper, faded to the colour of mud by industrial size washing machines and shrunk by the fierce heat of the tumble dryer. I could picture Annie shopping with her pal, Mary, looking for the perfect dress, just like the one they had seen Jean Harlow wearing in her latest film. It would cling in all the right places but leave enough to the imagination to create that sense of mystery, or so they thought. Jean Harlow wouldn't have been seen dead in the thin cotton frock that was eventually brought home in triumph.

Annie had a name and her memories but scarcely a hint of her real identity, the girl, the woman she used to be. Those Saturday nights at the dancing were real enough as if it was yesterday but if you asked Annie what she had for breakfast that morning she would probably say she hadn't had any. What happens to the memories that the brain cannot hold on to, I wonder, the occasional observer of lives lost in this last place of refuge. Sometimes I imagine that a spirit takes them away to store them for someone else, someone not yet born, who will live their life, reflecting the memory of that long ago girl. While the not-yet-born are waiting in the shadows the routines of the home provide safety and familiarity for the lost and sometimes the lonely whose world has shrunk to this place. No more shopping, dancing, love and waiting for the bus to go to the dancing, anticipation tingling in every pore. All that is left are the photos of faces that have not looked like that for years. I try to imagine what it must feel like to look at photos, faces, and not recognise them. Maybe there is a special place that some call the soul, that holds on to those memories. Or maybe they slowly wither and die, like the wretched bodies that reflect them.

Dinner time, the cutlery placed carelessly on the table by the harassed assistant, is a messy business. Even before the food arrives the other old woman, the unhappy recipient of this sad and difficult weekly visit, rearranges the cutlery and starts banging on the table with the spoon. I try to guess whether she is hungry, bored or angry. As the clatter of metal on wood gets louder and more insistent I try to remove the spoon. My reward is a sharp smack to the hand. This old wrinkled infant reminds me of a child in a highchair, playing a game. Her life now has the quality of demanding infancy, without the promise of change and growth. The only change here is into decay; a long, slow process in which all dignity is gone.

Annie is still weaving and moving to the music, smiling and lost in her world. Maybe she is remembering the boy she kissed before running up the close stairs to her mammy. I smile too, hoping that Annie enjoyed that kiss before her mammy caught her.

The Virgin And Her Pierced Red Heart
by Rosa MacPherson

The Virgin and her pierced red heart were waiting for me. She had a bouquet of flowers clutched to her bleeding breast and an outstretched hand, her finger towards me, beckoning. The hypnotic effect of her; the thorned beating breast of her: I was staring at hell inside Jesus' mam.

I had watched as the last of them left the church; the old man doubled, his cashmere tan coat buttoned to the chin; his fingers in the font, making a wet sign of the cross on his bent face; the little foreign mama in her black coat and bright scarf shaking her head; sad at something.

I'd stood at the side of the building; tilting my neck just enough to see them carefully latch the church gate behind them.

Then I slid inside.

The smell of candles, unlit now, and the incense lingered; ghosts remembered, chattered inside me. The incense spiralled memory and I giggled, nervously stepping between the pews, watching the cross in front; feeling the virgin's eyes on me from behind. I walked towards the unlocked door of the confessional and stepped inside. I let the voices out.

Bless me Father for I have sinned: I and Moses and his tablets of stone, striking this rock, this manna from heaven, these Ten Commandments. I have kept on taking your tablets. I have ordered this soul you gave me to be happy. But to no avail Lord. There is no happiness here. I have had to set my heart in stone just as your mother has done and as my mother has taught me to do. O bless us Lord. Have we indeed all sinned, your mam and mine and me?

Not a word in response. No burning bush, no piercing arrow, my face not shrouded in any divinity.

I stayed kneeled. Just in case. The light oak beneath my knees pressing.

The curtain in front of me closed; no live priest behind it. I wasn't going to look behind it. I knew there was no-one there. Father Gerard would be plonked in someone else's living room, drinking tea out of the best cup, murmuring yes yes of course, while staring at some poor unknowing daughter's tits like a dressed up exorcist at Halloween. Her mother smiling at him with her lipstick on.

I was breathless all of a sudden. Puffed out like when I'd run the cross country run to the Pleasure Grounds, gym-knickered and sweating. Waiting to see Father Gerard cross the pavilion, pretending not to see me.

Father Gerard the Bastard would be somewhere else right now. Not here in this church where the Lord God lives and his virgin mother bleeds, her bouquet of fresh lilies dripping onto her stone bare feet.

A person could lock themselves in here, on the inside of the confessional; keep the sinners out; the penance seekers waiting to do as they're told. Even I could serve a sentence here, if I was guilty of anything, which of course I'm not, except for my unhappiness with the Lord and the expectations he and everyone else has of me.

My knees begin to hurt and I lay my forehead onto the bar in front of the confessional opening. There are tears on my face and I let them drop, like virgin's blood.

Bless me Father for I have sinned. I have tried to be happy, like Doctor Taylor said. I take the tablets. And I have tried to follow my mother's instruction, to pray to you, Lord, not seek understanding, just accept the splitting of my virgin heart which no tablet can cure. I have tried to get used to it. To forget Father G's unholy face.

There was no way the Lord was listening. Mam was right. It's a man's world. I wiped the wet with the back of my hand and stepped out of the confessional into the aisle. The altar flowers were all white, the candles towering towards heaven. I knew that in the Sacristy, my mother's favourite place to pray, the Black Madonna's chapel would be polished brass, her dark face scarred and unwavering. The Virgin's other face.

Really.

The Bible doesn't tell us much about the virgin after Jesus died and her heart got broke. My mum tells me that's because God was inside her and she got over it and anyway she has eternity in heaven to make up for it.

I turn my back on the Black Madonna and look instead towards her virgin-white and starred-blue gaze. I look into her daggered heart and her stone stare.

If I stand here long enough I might see her heart beat.

Killing Time

by Dave Bisio

My Father killed Kennedy and Monroe.
He killed Sinatra and Picasso.
Committed murder. Kissed the sin.
Did them all. Was that assassin.

My Father killed Diana and Strumming Joe.
He killed Malcolm X and the Big O.
Stole each soul. Passed them away.
Hated their style. Loved to slay.

My Father killed Marley and James Dean.
He killed Lord Sutch and Steve McQueen.
Ended their lives. Broke every heart.
Dealt with the devil. Played out his part.

My Father killed Hendrix and Brando.
He killed John Wayne and Jill Dando.
Took the money. Did every hit.
Never wavered. Showed true grit.

My Father killed Lennon and Bruce Lee.
He killed Andy Warhol and Ian Dury.
He planned it all. Inside his head.
His mind came out. To claim the dead.

Unheard Voices - *An Anthology*

My Father killed Mercury and Marvin Gaye.
He killed Martin Luther and Man Ray.
Went really crazy. Became insane.
Had strange voices. Affected his brain.

My Father killed Elvis and Grace Kelly.
He killed Che Guevara and Buddy Holly.
Now he's killing time. In a secure place.
Taking his medicine. Getting lost in space.

Touching Peat

by Rosa MacPherson

I hadn't really touched you, you know. Oh, I felt your cool heat against the openness of my flat palm; your stray unfurling splinters of bark; hard hair beneath my fingers. I breathed your wetness.

But you, really, high up, here, with
the wind; gentle sometimes,
laying on this
earth, nothing stated,
nothing
held.
Nothing.

I didn't want to touch you, really,
try to make a mark on you. I
didn't want to enter
all those woods,

the slow unravelling layers; the dark; the inevitability. It was enough to be around you; outside of you, my arms wide, the world's breath even, deep, touching me, knowing everything was.

The moment filled me, warmed me, made me live through thousands of
years, through
grown seeds, sharp limbed trees rising and
falling, an eternal slow motion; layered star
cycles dying and birthing, murmuring silences weighing
everything.
And just being.

Here.
No place to hang words,
even
fine words, words that would
float
unhooked into
the soft breath , just
float
with the wind through the peat.

I couldn't touch you,
really. I didn't
even
want to try.

Just echoing
bones and stardust
pinned hopes
against the sky.

Further information about the Clackmannanshire writers-in-residence and up-coming writers' workshops can be found at the *Clackmannanshire Writers* website at www.clackswrite.org